TABLE OF CONTENTS

THIS PAGE INTENTIONALLY LEFT BLANK

LIST OF ACRONYMS AND ABBREVIATIONS

ACLU	American Civil Liberties Union
BOSS	Biometric Optical Surveillance System
CCTV	Closed Circuit Television
DARPA	Defense Advanced Research Projects Agency
FBI	Federal Bureau of Investigation
FRT	Facial Recognition Technology
GPS	Global Positioning System
IAFIS	Integrated Automated Fingerprint Identification System
NGI	Next Generation Identification

THIS PAGE INTENTIONALLY LEFT BLANK

ACKNOWLEDGMENTS

This work was made possible with the love and support of many. My wife, Tawana, and sons, Keegan and Connor, endured the long working hours with loving support and endless patience. My advisor, Professor Halladay, helped me find focus in the vastness of this field and provided great insight and mentoring about both the subject material and academic process. Thanks to my second reader, Professor Dahl, who shared his enthusiasm and inquisitiveness about privacy and surveillance and their effects on society. There are numerous other friends and colleagues who also provided help and support. To all, thank you.

THIS PAGE INTENTIONALLY LEFT BLANK

I. INTRODUCTION

In June 2001, in Ybor City, a suburb of Tampa, Florida, city administrators and police took part in a project that would divide the city on the issues of privacy and security. Using the already installed closed circuit television system in the downtown area, police installed a so-called "smart CCTV" system. The smart CCTV was unique because it used facial recognition technology and real-time surveillance footage to identify people, walking along the public streets in downtown Ybor City. For many residents, the smart CCTV system represented a scene right out of George Orwell's *1984,* where Big Brother watched every move of the citizens and privacy did not exist. To the police, it demonstrated an innovative approach to keeping the community secure by proactively embracing new technology.

A. MAJOR RESEARCH QUESTION

Though the invasion of privacy in the home is the primary protection of the Fourth Amendment (*Katz v. U.S.*[1]), should the spirit of the Fourth Amendment be broadened to encompass the privacy of the identity of individuals in public? The competing interests of law enforcement professionals and privacy advocates provide an opportunity to study the increased use of technology in the field of surveillance, its effects on privacy expectations, and existing legal protections for people in public places. By considering public surveillance efforts currently in service, studying current privacy protections under the law, and reviewing public acceptance of surveillance technology, this thesis seeks to answer whether facial recognition surveillance violates Fourth Amendment privacy protections and to what extent, and whether law enforcement and government security professionals can use facial recognition surveillance for combatting crime while continuing to protect the public's privacy expectations.

---

1 Katz v. United States, 389 U.S. 347 (1967).

B. SIGNIFICANCE OF THE RESEARCH QUESTION

Senator Al Franken, chairman of the Senate Judiciary Subcommittee on Privacy, Technology, and the Law, has "serious concerns about facial recognition technology (FRT) and how it might shape the future of privacy." He points out in an open letter to Alan Tussy, the maker of NameTag, an app that uses FRT to scour the Internet for identifying information about the faces it scans, that facial recognition is unlike any biometric technology that has come before it:

> Unlike other biometric identifiers such as iris scans and fingerprints, facial recognition is designed to operate at a distance, without the knowledge or consent of the person being identified. Individuals cannot reasonably prevent themselves from being identified by cameras that could be anywhere-on a lamppost across the street, attached to an unmanned aerial vehicle, or, now, integrated into the eyewear of a stranger.[2]

Senator Franken's concerns are valid, and this thesis explores whether the law considers a person's facial image as private or public when they show their face in public places, while also considering the ease with which modern technology can obtain identities.

Government agencies employ different types of FRT. The FBI, for example, recently began a program that compares still-shot images with a facial image database. Technology such as that used in the Ybor City project used active surveillance and real-time identification. There is a distinct difference when it comes to the privacy debate relating to active surveillance that is not present, or not as prevalent, when considering the comparison of still shots or frame captures. This thesis will explore the privacy issues that arise from the use of FRT with active surveillance cameras that identify suspects in real-time.

The most recent controversy regarding facial recognition is the FBI's Next Generation Identification (NGI) database, which builds on the fingerprint database that

---

2 Al Franken to Kevin Alan Tussy, February 5, 2014, http://www.franken.senate.gov/?p=press_release&id=2699.

the FBI has maintained since 1924.[3] The FBI has estimated that the database will contain 52 million facial images in 2015.[4] These images will be of the type and quality that investigators can search using facial matching of photos captured either by still camera or frames of CCTV shots. Lawmakers and the public should debate the question about who owns the rights to peoples' facial images, the image takers, or the owners of the face, considering the growing database of facial images that government agents can search at the lightning-quick speed of technology. This debate is relevant because facial images are no longer just snapshots taken in public, but potentially roadmaps to a person's identity.

The advent of new technology like FRT brings a new paradigm to the debate about privacy and security because, until recently, people who displayed their faces in public relinquished a bit of privacy, but they still maintained a level of anonymity. With FRT, it is possible to identify people in public covertly and from a distance in real-time, thus negating the expectation of privacy through anonymity they once enjoyed.

C.   LITERATURE REVIEW

Facial recognition technology is an evolving field and authors are frequently publishing new literature in the realm of facial recognition. This thesis captures the latest publications in the field and FRT relates to privacy. Literature regarding privacy and surveillance in the United States is extensive. This literature review includes relevant publications regarding employment of technology in the field of facial recognition, as well as publications related to privacy and surveillance-related privacy concerns.

1.   Current Use of Facial Recognition Technology

Industrialized countries throughout the world are employing facial recognition technology on a limited basis. Canadians use facial recognition surveillance at racetracks and inside casinos to catch known cheaters, or for people with gambling addictions to

---

3 Fingerprints and other Biometrics, The Federal Bureau of Investigation, Accessed September 17, 2014, http://www.fbi.gov/about-us/cjis/fingerprints_biometrics.

4 Mia De Graf and Mark Prigg, "FBI Facial Recognition Database that can Pick You Out from a Crowd in CCTV Shots is now 'Fully Operational,'" *Mail Online,* September 15, 2014, http://www.dailymail.co.uk/news/article-2756641/FBI-facial-recognition-database-pick-crowd-CCTV-shots-fully-operational.html.

voluntarily sign up for a no-gambling list—using the technology as a kind of self-help program.[5] The U.S. military uses facial recognition and other biometric information overseas to identify criminals and terrorists.[6] Such other countries as Australia and Japan use facial recognition at border ports of entry for identifying visa fraud[7] or speeding immigration lines.[8] Police agencies in San Diego County, California, use facial recognition on handheld devices like smartphones for real-time identification of criminals.[9]

Active facial recognition surveillance is rarely used. Police have tried using it inside the United States on a limited basis with little success. Kelly A. Gates points out that in the Ybor City Smart CCTV project, privacy formed a concern of the public: "In the case of Ybor City, civil liberties did have some resonance in public discourse about police adoption of the new surveillance technology...In fact, the conflict and controversy over the Smart CCTV project underscores a long-standing tension inherent in liberal governance between 'the twin dangers of governing too much...and governing too little.'"[10] More officially, Tampa Police spokesman Tom Durkin said, "Police discontinued using the system 'because of the lack of arrests, not the privacy issues.'"[11] In fact, the Ybor City project failed to identify any criminals. The reason for the discontinued use of the system was based partly on what Gates says were "the successful

5 "OLG and Commissioner Cavoukian Announce State-of-the-Art Privacy-Protective Facial Recognition system," *Privacy by Design,* November 12, 2010, http://www.privacybydesign.ca/index.php/ olg-and-commissioner-cavoukian-announce-state-of-the-art-privacy-protective-facial-recognition-system/.

6 Thom Shanker, "To Track Militants, U.S. Has System That Never Forgets a Face," *New York Times,* July 13, 2011, http://www.nytimes.com/2011/07/14/world/asia /14identity.html?pagewanted=all&_r=0.

7 Samantha Maiden, "Biometric Security at Borders to Catch Visa Fraud," *The Daily Telegraph,* April 01, 2012, http://www.dailytelegraph.com.au/biometric-security-at-borders-to-catch-visa-fraud/story-e6freuy9-1226315240076?nk=25772438d874a12404ff8d05d585a121.

8 "Test of Facial ID Recognition System Begins at Airports," *The Ashai Shimbun,* August 07, 2012, http://ajw.asahi.com/article/behind_news/social_affairs/AJ201208070087.

9 The Center for Investigative Reporting, "Police use Face Scans in the Field: Privacy Advocates are Concerned with the Military-grade Influx," *U-T San Diego,* November 08, 2013, http://www.utsandiego.com/news/2013/nov/08/cir-facial-recognition-software-san-diego/.

10 Kelly A. Gates, *Our Biometric Future: Facial Recognition Technology and the Culture of Surveillance* (New York: New York University Press, 2011), 92.

11 Ibid., 94.

efforts of vocal opponents to define automated facial recognition as a technology that gives the police too much power."[12] The police insisted they discontinued the use of the system when the free trial ran out because it failed to identify a single person.

2.   Understanding Privacy and Surveillance

Significant literature exists regarding privacy, but scholars and authors have yet to agree on a narrow definition of the term. Wisconsin law professor Ken Gormley notes several leading "clusters" of privacy explanations in the past 100 years:

> Many scholars, dating back to Roscoe Pound in 1915, and Paul Freund in 1975, have viewed privacy as an expression of one's personality or personhood, focusing upon the right of the individual to define his or her essence as a human being. Second, closely akin to the "personhood" cluster, are those scholars such as Louis Henkin who have marked privacy within the boundaries of autonomy—the moral freedom of the individual to engage in his or her own thoughts, actions and decisions. A third cluster, typified by Alan Westin and Charles Fried, have seen privacy—at least in large part—in terms of citizens' ability to regulate information about themselves, and thus control their relationships with other human beings, such that individuals have the right to decide "when, how, and to what extent information about them is communicated to others." Finally, a fourth cluster of scholars have taken a more noncommittal, mix-and-match approach, breaking down privacy into two or three essential components, such as Ruth Gavison's "secrecy, anonymity and solitude," and the "repose, sanctuary and intimate decision."[13]

The fourth of Gormley's clusters, the "non-committal" cluster, include themes also mentioned by Alan Westin in *Privacy and Freedom*. They are: solitude, intimacy, anonymity, and reserve.[14] People generally practice solitude and intimacy in private, or in the home. On the other hand, people practice anonymity and, to a certain extent

---

12 Ibid., 95.

13 Ken Gormley, "One Hundred Years of Privacy," Wisconsin Law Review 1335 (1992), Accessed December 1, 2014, http://www.lexisnexis.com.libproxy nps.edu/lnacui2api/api/version1/getDocCui?lni=3S41-1BM0-00CW-H07W&csi=270944,270077,11059,8411&hl=t&hv=t&hnsd=f&hns=t&hgn=t&oc=00240&perma=true/.

14 Alan F. Westin, *Privacy and Freedom* (New York: Atheneum, 1970), 7, 20–1, 31.

reserve, in public and are, therefore inevitably affected by public surveillance.[15] Westin also examines the individual privacy themes and social processes that intrude on individual expectations of privacy, such as surveillance.[16]

Westin points out that in order for the government to conduct surveillance with the consent of the public, the government must show more than the fact that surveillance can solve a particular social problem. He writes: "The need must be serious enough to overcome the very real and presently rising risk of jeopardizing the public's confidence in its daily freedom from unreasonable invasions of privacy."[17]

Westin writes that one school of thought regarding surveillance is that monitoring our neighbors is society's method of ensuring that everyone is following established laws.[18] In a modern example, Kelly A. Gates credits Mark Andrejevic with the term, "lateral surveillance," noting that when people on social networking sites post photos of themselves, they are simply exhibiting themselves. However, Gates writes, "browsing, searching, and identifying the photos of others is a way of watching over them, a form of what Andrejevic refers to as 'peer-to-peer' or 'lateral-surveillance.'"[19]

In her book, *Taking Liberties: The War on Terror and the Erosion of American Democracy,* Susan N. Herman, President of the American Civil Liberties Union, addresses specifically how privacy and democracy are inherently connected and the framers of the Constitution realized this fact. She points out that the Framers penned the Fourth Amendment with privacy specifically in mind and the government essentially lowered the Fourth Amendment barrier to intrusion after 9/11. Chapters in the Patriot

---

[15] Donald R. Zoufal, "Someone to Watch Over Me?: Privacy and Governance Strategies for CCTV and Emerging Surveillance Technologies" (MA thesis, Naval Postgraduate School, 2008), 35, http://handle.dtic.mil/100.2/ADA480074.

[16] Westin, *Privacy and Freedom*, 7, 20–1, 31.

[17] Ibid., 370.

[18] Ibid., 20.

[19] Gates, *Our Biometric Future*, 147.

Act, she notes, progressively shifted Fourth Amendment protections away from the framer's intentions.[20]

Carl Friedrich credits Immanuel Kant with claiming that any act done with intentional secrecy must mean that the foundation of the act lay in immorality.[21] In large communities, such as an entire nation, the government assumes the task for monitoring peoples' actions in the form of policing and security. Therefore, when a community member commits an act public, he is essentially declaring to the public, through their representative government, that his actions are legitimate and he has nothing to hide. Daniel Solove addresses the nothing-to-hide argument in his book, *Nothing to Hide: The False Tradeoff between Privacy and Security.* Essentially, Solove points out that the nothing-to-hide argument only speaks to some problems and not others. Within the face of the nothing-to-hide argument, a narrow focus of privacy is undertaken, but when focusing on privacy in the larger sense, say beyond surveillance and disclosure, the nothing-to-hide argument does not stand.[22] Solove explains, "It represents a singular and narrow way of conceiving of privacy, and it wins by excluding consideration of the other problems often raised with government security measures."[23] Therefore, the notion privacy is much more complex than those who use the nothing-to-hide argument are generally prepared to discuss. The nothing-to-hide argument leaves many unanswered questions when faced with the entirety of privacy-related issues.

American jurist Richard A. Posner tells us that people tend to exaggerate the harms from government surveillance and when comparing privacy values to security from a terrorism-related death, privacy should lose and security should win.[24] Posner points out that while surveillance "imposes costs on innocent people because their

---

20 Susan N. Herman, *Taking Liberties: The War On Terror and the Erosion of American Democracy* (New York: Oxford University Press, 2011), 111.

21 Carl J. Friedrich, "Secrecy versus Privacy: The Democratic Dilemma," in *Privacy,* ed. J. Roland Pennock and John W. Chapman (New York: Atherton Press, 1971), 106.

22 Daniel J. Solove, *Nothing to Hide: The False Tradeoff between Privacy and Security* (New Haven: Yale University Press, 2011), 32.

23 Ibid., 32.

24 Richard A. Posner, *Not a Suicide Pact: The Constitution in a Time of National Emergency* (New York: Oxford University Press, 2006), 80.

privacy is compromised...the costs it imposes on terrorists are even steeper because it thwarts their plans utterly and places them at risk of capture or death."[25] When debating the privacy compromises associated with FRT and active surveillance, society must weigh the costs associated with foregoing anonymity in public versus the benefit of active crime prevention using the newest technology available. Judge Posner's views show up closer to the side of crime prevention, and not public anonymity, when placed on the sliding scale of privacy versus security.

The distinction between what is, or should be, public and what is, or should be, private compiles much of the debate surrounding privacy-defining case law. Protecting Americans' privacy expectations has been a focus, particularly of legal scholars, since the late 19th century. Many authors cite Warren and Brandeis as among the first to write about "the right to privacy" in their 1890 article of the same name, published in the *Harvard Law Review*. In the article, they contend that the law should "protect those persons with whose affairs the community has no legitimate concern, from being dragged into an undesirable and undesired publicity."[26] The Warren and Brandeis article focuses on the publication of peoples' private affairs. It also addresses legal protections and options for redress. Warren and Brandeis explain when people make their private information public, they cannot claim an injury when someone else makes the same information public. One may draw a conclusion then, that when people show their faces in public, the law should not consider any reproduction of those images a violation of their privacy.

3.   Social Evolution and Facial Recognition Technology

"Familiarity breeds acceptance."[27] These are the words of Susan N. Herman in her book, *Taking Liberties: The War on Terror and the Erosion of American Democracy*. Herman refers broadly to the security measures put in place after 9/11 that appear to

---

25 Richard A. Posner, "Privacy, Surveillance, and Law," *The University of Chicago Law Review* 75, no. 1 (2008): 246, URL: http://www.jstor.org/stable/20141907.

26 Samuel D. Warren and Louis D. Brandeis, "The Right to Privacy," *Harvard Law Review* 4, no. 5 (1890): 214, doi: 10.2307/1321160.

27 Herman, *Taking Liberties*, 85.

bolster security at the expense of liberty, but which have not been shown to produce much good in the way of security. For having acquiesced to these measures, however, American society is now stuck with them, whether or not they work—and even if the threat abates. She writes, "Once we become accustomed to a new baseline, like bag searches or body scanners at the airport, those practices, like the idea of watchlists, are likely to proliferate."[28] She continues by saying that we continue to employ these tactics without knowing their effectiveness: "By the laws of inertia, these and other security programs are likely to continue into a second decade even though we have no way of knowing whether they are worthwhile."[29] Thus, the public's familiarity with the security measures has bred an acceptance. Much in the same way that watchlists and body scanners have withstood the privacy advocates' concerns, so will FRT likely breed acceptance.

Kelly A. Gates notes that FRT is not a result of a post-9/11 world, as some would say. She claims that FRT is part of a natural progression of technology that would have come about regardless of 9/11. She explains that "according to the tech-neutrality view, pursuit of these technologies need not be understood as part of a particular security strategy, since they are products of the natural progression of science and technology, part of the inevitable unfolding process of computerization."[30] The employment of facial recognition surveillance is an inevitable progression of security technology. As people become more accustomed to the technology, it will be more accepted and more widely used. Just as Warren and Brandeis were concerned that photographs printed in the paper of people's doings in public would ruin privacy by shouting their business from the rooftops seems ridiculous to us now, so will concerns about facial recognition surveillance seem ridiculous to the general public in the future.

Some privacy advocates believe the potential for government abuse of surveillance technology exists and current privacy protections under the law do not allow for the use of technology like facial recognition surveillance. Law professor Susan

---

28 Ibid.

29 Ibid.

30 Gates, *Our Biometric Future*, 197.

Freiwald writes, "The courts have...identified a four-factor test that identifies when a surveillance method intrudes on Fourth Amendment rights and requires heightened judicial oversight to protect against abuse."[31] The four-factor test of clandestine, intrusive, continuous, and indiscriminate surveillance requires that government agencies should obtain a warrant before using technology that would allow individual tracking. The warrant requirement reduces the opportunity for abuse by providing judicial oversight. It is clear, through an examination of case law, that many questions of privacy intrusions on the part of the government would never have come to light had a warrant application by the police, and issuance by a magistrate, occurred before the privacy injury. But it is through the lens of these cases that we begin to visualize a more precise indication of society's privacy expectations.

4. Constitutional and Legal Protections

Although the word *privacy* does not appear in the Constitution, there is still legal protection for it. An examination of case law enforces this point. Privacy was described in *United States v. Blok*[32] as "one of the unique values of our civilization." Privacy exists not only in case law, but in the assumptions of most Americans. They believe they have privacy, therefore Americans must take privacy expectations into account when deciding how, or if, a privacy violation has occurred in a particular case. Although the word privacy does not appear in the Constitution, the expectations of privacy that Americans believe they possess comprise the core of most privacy-related jurisprudence.

Privacy protections reside primarily in cases relating to the Fourth Amendment, which protects people and their homes from unwarranted search and seizure. The primary case involving the interpretation of privacy relating to the Fourth Amendment is *Katz v. United States*.[33] In *Katz*, the F.B.I. placed a microphone and recording device on a telephone booth where they knew their suspect would likely later place a phone call to commit the crime of interstate wagering. It was determined in the *Katz* decision that a

---

31 Susan Freiwald, "The Four Factor Test," *The Selected Works of Susan Freiwald*, 2013, http://works.bepress.com/susan_freiwald/11.

32 United States v. Blok, 188 F. 2d 1019 - Court of Appeals, Dist. of Columbia Circuit (1951).

33 Katz v. United States, 389 U.S. 347 (1967).

person has a reasonable expectation of privacy in a public telephone booth and that technology, employed by the government without a warrant that "listens" to the conversation inside the booth, constitutes an illegal search, even if the device did not penetrate the interior of the space, because the Fourth Amendment protects people, not places.

A public expectation of privacy also figured in *Oliver v. United States,*[34] where police officers conducted a search of an open field. In *Oliver,* the court held that "human relations that create the need for privacy do not ordinarily take place in open fields." One could argue the same for public monitoring using FRT. Courts have held that people have no expectation of privacy when it comes to being seen in public.

Also at issue is the question of whether government surveillance for the purpose of national security is relevant to the privacy argument. The President of the United States is responsible under Art. II, § 1, of the Constitution, to "preserve, protect and defend the Constitution of the United States." This requirement implies a duty to protect against those who would illegally disrupt or overthrow the government. In *U.S. v. U.S. District Court for the Eastern District of Michigan et al.,* known commonly as the *Keith* case, it was noted that, "the President–through the Attorney General – may find it necessary to employ electronic surveillance to obtain intelligence information on the plans of those who plot unlawful acts against the Government. The use of such surveillance in internal security cases has been sanctioned more or less continuously by various Presidents and Attorneys General since July 1946."[35]

In 1965, President Johnson appointed a Commission on Law Enforcement and Administration of Justice, which was later named the "Crime Commission." The Crime Commission found that the use of electronic surveillance by law enforcement was instrumental to thwarting organized crime: "The great majority of law enforcement officials believe that the evidence necessary to bring criminal sanctions to bear consistently on the higher echelons of organized crime will not be obtained without the

---

34 Oliver v. United States, 466 U.S. 170 (1984).

35 United States v. United States District Court for the Eastern District of Michigan et al. (Plamondon et al., real parties in interest), 407 U.S. 297 (1972).

aid of electronic surveillance techniques. They maintain these techniques are indispensable to develop adequate strategic intelligence concerning organized crime, to set up specific investigations, to develop witnesses, to corroborate their testimony, and to serve as substitutes for them—each a necessary step in the evidence-gathering process in organized crime investigations and prosecutions."[36] The *Keith* case showed that while electronic surveillance was important for law enforcement officials in the protection of national security, the police must conduct intentional electronic surveillance directed at a specific person or persons with sufficient judicial oversight. That is, they must first obtain a warrant.

Illinois v. Lidster[37] is an important case relating to unwarranted and public surveillance. In the case, the police were conducting a traffic checkpoint to identify the suspect in a fatal hit and run accident. *Lidster* held that using surveillance to catch a suspect was more important than the privacy of the other people whom the police subjected to the surveillance. Judge Posner wrote, "*Lidster* is important because it divorces searching from suspicion. It allows surveillance that invades liberty and privacy to be conducted because of the importance of the information sought, even if it is not sought for use in a potential criminal proceeding against the people actually under surveillance."[38]

In *Kyllo v. U.S.,*[39] the United States Supreme Court reviewed a case to decide whether the use of technology to peer into a person's home constituted a search of the home. In the *Kyllo* case, police used a thermal imaging device from a public street to essentially see beyond the walls of a private residence and detect the amount of heat emanating from the residence to determine if heat lamps typically used for growing marijuana might be in use inside the home.

An important aspect of the *Kyllo* case was that the use of thermal imaging technology was not revealing private acts in a private place, but simply a change in

---

[36] Ibid.

[37] Illinois v. Lidster, 540 U.S. 419 (2004).

[38] Posner, *Not a Suicide Pact*, 91.

[39] Kyllo v. U.S., 533 U.S. 27 (2001).

temperature from one part of the house to the next. The court found, however, that the Fourth Amendment protected any details, however slight, when obtained from the home using the new technology, and the police were required to obtain a search warrant.

Another topic to note regarding *Kyllo* is the court distinguished that the public did not generally use thermal imaging technology, nor was it readily available for off-the-shelf operation. When it comes to FRT, the public, for a large part, knowingly participates in employing and improving facial recognition. Kelly A. Gates points out in her book, *Our Biometric Future: Facial Recognition Technology and the Culture of Surveillance,* that the public uses the FRT provided by social networking sites such as Facebook to manage their personal photos.[40]

The U.S. Supreme Court left a question unanswered in *United States v. Knotts,*[41] when deciding a case where the police tracked an electronic monitoring device inside a package without a warrant. The question left unanswered was whether monitoring the package, which the police could not track visually, constituted a search using technology. Facial recognition technology conducts the same investigation as, for example, a police officer on the street. At the beginning of a shift, if a police officer reviews photographs of wanted criminals before taking to the streets, he has in his head a database of faces from which to compare the people he sees in public. In the same way, FRT sees faces in public and either identifies them as a wanted criminal or not. The difference is that the camera and database of FRT are much more efficient than a police officer. This thesis will explore the question of whether the efficiency increase provided by technology violates privacy expectations of people in public.

D.   POTENTIAL EXPLANATIONS AND HYPOTHESIS

The leading hypothesis of this thesis is that use of facial recognition surveillance by law enforcement agencies and government security specialists does not violate privacy protections under the Fourth Amendment.

---

40 Gates, *Our Biometric Future*, 136–7.

41 *United States v. Knotts,* 460 U. S. 276 (1983).

There are existing legal protections for privacy. The law has considered and allowed public surveillance for many years.[42] However, emerging technologies allow for massive surveillance, in real time, and also allow operators to save and access the results of the surveillance again at a later time. While emerging technology, such as facial recognition, presents an incredible opportunity for law enforcement and government security professionals to locate, track, and associate criminals and terrorists, the potential for abuse also exists. Privacy advocates recognize the potential for abuse and warn against the unrestricted use of FRT.

E.   RESEARCH DESIGN

This thesis examines existing protections under current U.S. law through case analyses and legal writings. Additionally, I examine circumstances where authors have debated emerging technology and privacy. This thesis contains an analysis of available works relating to advancing technology and the progression of social concerns through court interpretations. Also, I look at the acceptance of technology intruding into the individual and societal realms of privacy through an examination of existing peer-reviewed works, published books, and relevant periodicals. I also compare the same privacy issues faced with the expanded use of what was another new technology, CCTV.

F.   THESIS OVERVIEW

This thesis begins with a non-technical overview of the technological advancement and use of FRT. I draw a distinction between active surveillance using FRT and using the technology for still shots taken from cameras. Next, this thesis studies the themes associated with privacy especially concerning surveillance. There are several privacy aspects to explore, but there are two in particular that relate to public surveillance, anonymity, and reserve. Surveillance of the public is not a new concept and there are existing laws governing surveillance methods and procedures. Finally, a thorough analysis of constitutional and legal protections is examined with regard to privacy and surveillance, both before and after the dawn of the digital age, and a

---

42 Christopher Slobogin, *Privacy at Risk: The New Government Surveillance and the Fourth Amendment* (Chicago: University of Chicago Press, 2007), 3.

14

determination is made as to whether Fourth Amendment privacy protections are violated by facial recognition surveillance.

THIS PAGE INTENTIONALLY LEFT BLANK

II. OVERVIEW OF FACIAL RECOGNITION TECHNOLOGY

Facial recognition technology has been researched and employed on a limited basis inside the United States from around the mid- to late-20th century—with a poor record of success. The equipment and software required to successfully employ FRT has not been widely effective at providing the kinds of results that agencies and operators have desired from the technology. Research in the United States, aimed at programming computers for recognizing human faces, began with the military in the 1960s, but it was not until the 1990s that commercial interest took hold in the field of facial recognition.[43]

Most people in the U.S. are accustomed to public monitoring for security reasons.[44] Although there is an accepted level of monitoring people tolerate, the level of acceptance is predicated on anonymity. Author Kimberly Brown wrote, "People...expect to go about daily life in relative obscurity—unidentifiable to others they do not already know, do not care to know, or are not required to know—so long as they abide by the law."[45] Facial recognition technology has the potential for removing anonymity from public surveillance thus degrading the level of privacy people experience in public.

FRT uses facial characteristics to identify and correlate such "nodal points" on a face as the eyes, nose, chin, cheekbones, etc. Software then compares these points to each other and compiles into a profile or faceprint. The software uses things like pores, wrinkles, and spots to further enhance the profile. The faceprints are stored in a database that the program can then search for matching profiles.[46]

---

43 Gates, *Our Biometric Future*, 27.

44 Dana Blanton, "Fox News Poll: Mixed views on NSA surveillance program," *Foxnews.com*, June 25, 2013, http://www.foxnews.com/politics/2013/06/25/fox-news-poll-mixed-views-on-nsa-surveillance-program/.

45 Kimberly N. Brown, "Article: Anonymity, Faceprints, and the Constitution," *George Mason Law Review*, Winter (2014): 2.

46 Ibid.

FRT took a leap forward in the 21st century, especially after the attacks of September 11. Recent advances in real-time FRT surveillance appear promising, but researchers have labeled the technology as *still inadequate for practical use*.[47]

A.   EARLY HISTORY OF FRT

The early beginnings of FRT trace back to the 1960s where both military and civilian scientists worked to create a technology that could prove useful on the battlefield. Scientists who originally conceived of the technology thought it could potentially, "identify, at a distance, specific individuals among the enemy ranks."[48]

Companies competed in the 1960s for computer-related research grants from the Defense Advanced Research Projects Agency (DARPA). Among the research areas was facial pattern recognition in photographs. The applicability of the emerging technology was not entirely defined, but Manuel De Landa wrote, "[T]he idea was not to transfer human skills to a machine, but to integrate humans and machines so that the intellectual skills of the former could be amplified by the latter."[49]

During the sixties, Panoramic Research Inc.'s co-founder Woodrow Wilson Bledsoe discovered the unique problems associated with FRT that still plague the FRT community today.[50] Upon developing a facial recognition program that was heavily reliant on human interfacing, Bledsoe found that stock images used in facial recognition database searches must have a set of high-quality characteristics to produce a searchable product. Those important characteristics, which still hinder the advancement of FRT today, five decades later, are: "head rotation and tilt, lighting intensity and angle, facial expression, aging, etc."[51]

---

47 Charlie Savage, "Facial Scanning is Making Gains in Surveillance," *The New York Times,* August 21, 2013, accessed October 10, 2014, http://www.nytimes.com/2013/08/21/us/facial-scanning-is-making-gains-in-surveillance.html?pagewanted=all.

48 Gates, *Our Biometric Future*, 29.

49 Ibid.

50 Ibid., 30.

51 Ibid.

Gaining from the research conducted in the 1960s, scientists in the 1970s sought to take out the requirement for heavy human-interaction in detecting a facial form in photographs. A couple of advances by researchers at Stanford University in California, and Kyoto University in Japan, led to increased abilities for computer software to identify facial forms in photographs. The limited successes in the field of FRT through the mid-1980s led scientists to focus on more limited goals rather than the coveted idea of real-time identification that was the desired end-state from the original conception of the technology.[52]

Until recently, scientists have struggled with the original set of problems faced by Bledsoe in the 1960s. For FRT to accurately identify a person, an amalgam of distinct characteristics needed to be present in a photograph. Those circumstances largely have not changed. Technological advancements in the fields of photography and videography, however have facilitated better opportunities for stock images, worthy of facial recognition, to appear in image databases.[53]

B.   RECENT ADVANCES IN FRT

The terrorist attacks of 9/11 demonstrated to the American public that although the end of the Cold War left the United States without a peer competitor in the realm of major military powers, the new enemies of the United States represented "asymmetric threats." "Unidentifiable" enemies made the nation vulnerable. Gates recounts, "The United States may no longer have an enemy that could match its military might…but it now has more insidious enemies that do not play by the conventional rules of state warfare, and thus represent significant threats to the nation, disproportionate to their relatively minuscule military resources."[54] One idea became popular for identifying the new threats. It was something that America did very well: technological development. Information technology companies and security brokers went to work developing

---

52 Gates, *Our Biometric Future*, 29–31.

53 Federal Trade Commission, "FTC Recommends Best Practices for Companies That Use Facial Recognition Technologies," October 22, 2012, http://www.ftc.gov/news-events/press-releases/2012/10/ftc-recommends-best-practices-companies-use-facial-recognition.

54 Gates, *Our Biometric Future*, 99.

technologies that would assist the United States with identifying their new enemies. Gates explains:

> In the language of cultural studies, the aftermath of 9/11 was a moment of articulation, where objects or events that have no necessary connection come together and a new discursive formation is established: automated facial recognition as a homeland security technology, a means of automatically identifying the faces of "terrorists." The interests of biometrics industry brokers to push their technologies after 9/11 translated well into the prevailing public policy and press response to the attacks: the frenzied turn to "security experts" to speculate as to the source of the security failures and to provide recommendations for "stopping the next one."[55]

Americans saw FRT as an opportunity to both play to their strengths in technological development and locate the elusive terrorists that were the target of their newest conflict.

There was an American preoccupation with facial recognition after 9/11. The idea that FRT could identify terrorist suspects in public locations before they commit their crimes was the answer to the "asymmetric threats" and "unidentifiable enemies" problems. Visionics, an early developer of FRT, used 9/11 as a springboard for a funding campaign. Shortly after the attacks, Visionics claimed that the only obstacle to fully successful employment of FRT surveillance was federal funding.[56] In fact, there were many competing biometrics industries vying for funding in the immediate post-9/11 security problem-solving age.

Lisa Nelson writes that the biometrics industry was fragmented and disorganized—it needed an overarching authority to bring organization coherency to the industry in order to focus efforts and work toward a more comprehensive security solution: "As quickly became clear, biometric technology encompasses myriad technologies, each with its own set of weaknesses. Instead of one coherent technology, the biometric industry was a series of industries within an industry."[57] She continues:

---

55 Gates, *Our Biometric Future*, 100.

56 Lisa S. Nelson, *America Identified* (Cambridge, MA: The MIT Press, 2011), 68.

57 Ibid., 69.

"Certainly the lack of stability and coherence in the industry might have been endemic to any technology reaching technological maturity; however, these factors added to the issue for decision makers in the aftermath of September 11."[58] What the biometrics industry needed was a central organization from which to build cohesiveness—preferably one that already existed.

A clear answer to the problem of a fractured biometrics collection and retention lay in the FBI's Integrated Automated Fingerprint Identification System (IAFIS).[59] The FBI had been collecting biometrics, such as fingerprints, for decades and the database presented a central location to store and access advances in biometric identifiers. More than a decade later, at a cost of many millions of dollars, the FBI now has a new system, called Next Generation Identification, acting as a repository for such biometric information as fingerprints, iris scans, palm prints, tattoos, and faceprints.[60]

The FBI's Next Generation Identification (NGI) database contains approximately 400 million facial images.[61] Ten states have granted the FBI access to their driver's license and state identification card photograph databases.[62] Thirty-seven states are using FRT for investigations that take minutes now compared to what may have taken hundreds of hours to manually complete.[63] Some investigators are able to access FRT databases in the field via their patrol car data terminals or even smart phones.[64] Investigations using this type of FRT are worrying to some privacy advocates because of the information sharing and speed with which investigations can take place. However, more troubling to privacy advocates than photograph database access is the immediate identification of people in public places using active facial recognition surveillance.

---

[58] Nelson, *America Identified*, 69.

[59] Ibid., 71.

[60] The FBI Federal Bureau of Investigation, "Next Generation Identification," accessed November 15, 2014, http://www.fbi.gov/about-us/cjis/fingerprints_biometrics/ngi.

[61] Brown, "Anonymity," 8.

[62] Ibid.

[63] Ibid.

[64] Ali Winston, "Facial recognition, once a battlefield tool, lands in San Diego County," *The Center for Investigative Reporting,* November 7, 2013, accessed November 19, 2013, http://cironline.org/reports/facial-recognition-once-battlefield-tool-lands-san-diego-county-5502#.

To date, the system nearest to being able to identify faces in a crowd using real-time surveillance is the Biometric Optical Surveillance System (BOSS). Developed through funding from the Department of Homeland Security, BOSS is still in production and testing, but according to a recent article by Ginger McCall in *The New York Times,* "The BOSS, if completed, will use video cameras to scan people in public (or will be fed images of people from other sources) and then identify individuals by their faces, presumably by cross-referencing databases of driver's license photos, mug shots or other facial images cataloged by name."[65]

The BOSS technology is quite powerful and evokes emotions in people reminiscent of the mass surveillance experienced by the Orwellian society of Oceania in the book *1984,* where Big Brother was potentially watching every move, made by anyone, at any time.[66] One difference between Oceania in *1984,* and the BOSS, is that images and associated locations may be stored for access in later investigations. This invites what some have called potential abuses. McCall writes: "While this sort of technology may have benefits for law enforcement (recall that the suspects in the Boston Marathon bombings were identified with help from camera footage), it also invites abuse. Imagine how easy it would be, in a society increasingly videotaped and monitored on closed-circuit television, for the authorities to identify antiwar protesters or Tea Party marchers and open dossiers on them, or for officials to track the public movements of ex-lovers or rivals. 'Mission creep' often turns crime-fighting programs into instruments of abuse."[67] For example, mission creep would be to use the data obtained by BOSS in a way that employing agency had not originally intended or sanctioned. Mission creep and data security are of particular concern to those who would not normally consider themselves targets of police investigations.

Facial recognition technology has the potential to greatly enhance policing and government security efficiency in the United States. The advancement of FRT could

---

65 Ginger McCall, "The Face Scan Arrives," *The New York Times,* August 30, 2013, http://www.nytimes.com/2013/08/30/opinion/the-face-scan-arrives html?_r=0.

66 George Orwell, *Nineteen Eighty-Four* (New York: Harcourt, Brace, 1949), 5.

67 McCall, "The Face Scan Arrives."

potentially accomplish in seconds what would take hundreds or thousands of man-hours to complete manually. The decades-long development of FRT is coming to a point where, in the near future, personal information about people can be so quickly accessed that their identity, location, and other personal information can be determined and logged within seconds. This technology, if left unregulated by law, should be particularly troubling to those who have no reason to be concerned with law enforcement surveillance.

THIS PAGE INTENTIONALLY LEFT BLANK

III.   PRIVACY AND SURVEILLANCE

Facial recognition technology contributes to an Orwellian society that many fear is transforming through technological advances in surveillance. Technological advancement of facial recognition technology bridged with uploaded photos on social networking, driver's licenses, unmanned aerial drones, public surveillance cameras, and police body-cameras threatens anonymity. All of these surveillance databases combined with the FBI's NGI, and other bits and bytes available in the public domain, can create an intimate profile of the daily life of a person who believes they are remaining anonymous in public.[68]

Privacy advocates are concerned with the unwitting, or unwilling, participation in privacy-invading activities that facial recognition forces on people appearing in public. As Senator Franken pointed out, FRT does not allow a person to actively participate in monitoring or identification.[69] Privacy and surveillance are at odds when linked with FRT and current protections under the law.

A.   PRIVACY

Active surveillance in public using facial recognition technology can serve to degrade anonymity and reserve, thus robbing individuals of the comfort associated with maintaining their personal privacy. The desire to remain anonymous to the government has a history dating back to the Founding.[70] The advent of technologies, such as FRT, has eroded the ability of Americans to remain anonymous and creates the possibility of future harms.[71] The themes of anonymity and reserve are most important when examining the effects of surveillance technology on privacy in modern America because they deal with individuals' interactions within society.[72]

---

[68] Brown, "Anonymity," 2.

[69] Al Franken to Kevin Alan Tussy, February 5, 2014, http://www.franken.senate.gov/?p=press_release&id=2699.

[70] Brown, "Anonymity," 2.

[71] Ibid.

[72] Westin, *Privacy and Freedom*, 31–2.

1.   Anonymity

Anonymity is "when the individual is in public places or performing public acts but still seeks, and finds, freedom from identification and surveillance."[73] A person in public, "does not expect to be personally identified and held to the full rules of behavior and role that would operate if he were known to those observing him. In this state the individual is able to merge into the 'situational landscape.'"[74] The employment of FRT by government security agencies and police may have a profound effect on the condition of anonymity because a person being watched by FRT is not only under surveillance in public, potentially without their knowledge or consent, but they are also subject to identification without their knowledge or consent.

People act and feel differently in public when they know they will remain anonymous. Removing the feeling of anonymity "destroys the sense of relaxation and freedom that men seek in open spaces and public arenas."[75] This destruction of peace is the first of three harms associated with compromised anonymity according to author Kimberly Brown in the *George Mason Law Review*:[76] adverse influence on behavior, emotional harm, and reduced accountability for the *watchers*. People experience emotional harm, as described by Westin, when the knowledge of surveillance destroys "relaxation and freedom." People experience stress and the inability to relax. The result of monitoring can affect their social interactions.[77]

Self-regulating behavior, in the form of censorship, can develop, whether voluntarily or involuntarily, as a result of surveillance.[78] There exists a possibility for abuse through manipulation and controlling peoples' behavior through the social norms that develop as a result of long-term surveillance.[79] A fear of retaliation cultivates that

---

[73] Ibid.

[74] Ibid.

[75] Ibid.

[76] Brown, "Anonymity," 10.

[77] Ibid.

[78] Brown, "Anonymity," 10.

[79] Ibid.

can lead people in a democratic society to forego objecting to policies with which they disagree. Brown notes, "The pressures of having one's private scandals 'outed' can push people toward socially influenced courses of action that without public disclosure and discussion, would never happen. They are less willing to voice controversial ideas or associate with fringe groups for fear of bias or reprisal."[80]

Modern surveillance, such as FRT, involves creating massive databases and reduces privacy security. Massive searchable databases create the "aggregation effect," according to Daniel J. Solove.[81] In effect, data about a person that is available with minimal effort through the use of computer searches makes the compilation of that data "vastly more than the sum of its parts."[82] Solove demonstrates the aggregation effect by comparing it with the pointillism paintings of Seurat. "Similar to a Seurat painting, where a multitude of dots juxtaposed together form a picture, bits of information when aggregated paint a portrait of a person."[83]

When a person is unknowingly subjected to FRT, their faceprint is combined with other data about them, thus revealing new information about which the subject has no knowledge or control over. This could be particularly troubling if the FRT operator uses the information in a negative way. Brown adds, "The party doing the aggregating gains a powerful tool for forming and disseminating personal judgments that render the subject vulnerable to public humiliation and other tangible harms, including criminal investigation."[84]

2. Reserve

Reserve, according to Westin's themes, is the fourth state of privacy. It is the ability for discretion where a person decides what they want to share with others and

---

[80] Brown, "Anonymity,"10 (quoting Jeffrey Rosen, *The Purposes of Privacy: A Response,* 89 GEO. L.J. 2117, 2122 (2001).

[81] Solove, *Digital Person,* 44.

[82] Solove, *Digital Person,* 44 (quoting Julie E. Cohen, "DRM and Privacy," 18 Berkeley Tech. L.J., 575–585 (2003).

[83] Solove, *Digital Person,* 44.

[84] Brown, "Anonymity," 10.

what they want to keep for themselves. Reserve was first established around the turn of the 20th century, when Warren and Brandeis penned their *Harvard Law Review* article stating that the information to be shared about a person should be under that person's control, and the subject should retain the "right to be let alone." Gormley references Professor Hyman Gross in explaining the importance and personal nature reserve has on privacy:

> It is through this delicate process of "editorial privilege" that we establish our identities in a social setting, thus maintaining control over how society views us: as parents, brothers and sisters, employers, employees, neighbors, citizens, all of the different roles and perceptions which collectively establish our identity, and individuality, within a modern American democracy. As a legally protected right, the original species of privacy introduced by Warren and Brandeis can be defined as the "right to be let alone, with respect to the acquisition and dissemination of information concerning the person, particularly through unauthorized publication, photography, or media."[85]

Reserve is important in personal relationships, but reserve also has a function in public. Westin notes: "The manner in which individuals claim reserve, and the extent to which it is respected or disregarded by others, is at the heart of securing meaningful privacy in the crowded, organization-dominated settings of modern industrial society and urban life."[86]

Keeping identities and personal information and about one's activities away from the public are important privacy concerns affected by employing FRT. Westin wrote that in order for a community to accept surveillance, the need for surveillance, "must be serious enough to overcome the very real and presently rising risk of jeopardizing the public's confidence in its daily freedom from unreasonable invasions of privacy."[87]

---

[85] Gormley, "One Hundred Years."

[86] Westin, *Privacy and Freedom*, 32.

[87] Ibid., 370.

B.   SURVEILLANCE

Simply put, surveillance is monitoring people for the possibility of social intervention.[88] Public and private organizations are increasingly installing surveillance cameras for deterrence and/or investigative purposes.[89] But passive surveillance systems can be improved by identifying the people they are recording and, hopefully, identifying a threat before a crime is committed. Facial recognition technology makes this improvement possible.

David Murakami Wood gave an important and comprehensive definition of surveillance in *A Report on the Surveillance Society*, to the United Kingdom's Information Commissioner in 2006. Wood stated that rather than using a government-generated definition for surveillance, a detailed look at the process is necessary: "Where we find purposeful, routine, systematic and focused attention paid to personal details, for the sake of control, entitlement, management, influence or protection, we are looking at surveillance."[90]

Wood introduces the important notion that surveillance is not simply watching and recording, but making identifications and using the information gathered. Facial recognition surveillance provides the identification piece of surveillance introduced by Wood. The identification of individuals by their face and how that information is, or will be, used is a concern of privacy advocates.

The widespread proliferation of video surveillance devices and people's uninhibited sharing of personal information through social media have created a culture of acceptance for potentially privacy-violating technology to be employed by government agencies and the longer this unchecked theme continues, the harder it will become for privacy advocates to justifiably call for intervention. The enhanced information sharing

---

[88] Sean P. Hier and Josh Greenberg, *Surveillance: Power, Problems, and Politics* (Vancouver: UBC Press, 2009), ix.

[89] Roy Coleman and Michael McCahill, *Surveillance and Crime* (Thousand Oaks, CA: Sage Publications Ltd., 2011), 98.

[90] David Murakami Wood, ed., "A Report on the Surveillance Society: Full Report," Report for the Information Commissioner by the Surveillance Studies Network (London, United Kingdom 2006), https://ico.org.uk/about_us/research/~/media/documents/library/Data_Protection/Practical_application/ Surveillance_Society_Full_Report_2006.ashx.

between government agencies and voluntary mass-oversharing of the unsuspecting public combine systems and information to create a vulnerability for a "totalitarian repression" as described by Hier and Greenberg:

> No government—totalitarian or broadly democratic—has ever had at its fingertips the surveillance infrastructure capacity that is unwittingly being created by the countless localized decisions to augment visibility. As the public has become inured to repeated warnings about "Big Brother," and seduced by the assorted abilities of new surveillance technologies, what prospect is there to champion a political effort to foreground the prospects of unequalled totalitarian repression that lies dormant within emergent surveillance structures?[91]

Reginald Whitaker, who coined the term *Little Brother*—referring to government control and censoring of the Internet—recognized the potential danger in turning over too much information-controlling power to the government.[92] This cry went out in 1999, before the advent of social networking, selfies, and mass Internet over-sharing. Sixteen years of increasingly revealing personal information sharing online has led to an increased capacity for government surveillance, but we have yet to see wide-spread totalitarian repression as postulated by Hier and Greenberg.

Government agencies frequently use surveillance to preempt danger. Some are concerned that, if left unchecked, governments will use preemption to justify mass surveillance where everyone is watched all the time.[93] Maureen Webb notes in her book, *Illusions of Security: Global Surveillance and Democracy in the Post-9/11 World,* that the G-8 countries (Canada, France, Germany, Italy, Japan, Russia, United Kingdom, and United States) have established a global infrastructure for mass registration and surveillance of entire populations. They consist of various initiatives that, when viewed collectively seem to, "aim to ensure that almost everyone on the planet is 'registered,' that all travel is tracked globally, that all electronic communications and transactions are monitored or accessible to the state, and that all information collected about individuals

---

[91] Hier and Greenberg, *Power, Problems, and Politics*, xviii.

[92] Reginald Whitaker, *The End of Privacy: How Total Surveillance Is Becoming a Reality* (New York: New Press, 1999), 111–5.

[93] Maureen Webb, *Illusions of Security: Global Surveillance and Democracy in the Post-9/11 World* (San Francisco: City Lights Books, 2007), 69.

in public and private sector databases is stored, linked, data-mined, and made available to state agents."[94]

1.   Panopticon

This type of mass surveillance monitoring, without overt public knowledge or consent, smacks of Bentham's Panopticon. Actually, the idea owes as much to Michel Foucault, who re-introduced Bentham's Panopticon in his book *Discipline and Punish*, in 1977. Bentham wrote about the Panopticon more than a century earlier, but it was Foucault's origination of *panopticism* that brought Bentham's Panopticon to the attention of more than just philosophy, history, and political science scholars.[95] A Panopticon is a surveillance design where the watcher has the capability, and presents the illusion, of watching multiple subjects at any or all times without the subjects knowing they are being watched. Foucault describes Bentham's Panopticon and the major effect:

> The major effect of the Panopticon: to induce in the inmate a state of conscious and permanent visibility that assures the automatic functioning of power. So to arrange things that the surveillance is permanent in its effects, even if it is discontinuous in its action; that the perfection of power should tend to render its actual exercise unnecessary; that this architectural apparatus should be a machine for creating and sustaining a power relation... [such that] the inmates should be caught up in a power situation of which they are themselves the bearers. In view of this, Bentham laid down the principle that power should be visible and unverifiable...in the peripheric ring, one is totally seen, without ever seeing; in the central tower, one sees everything without ever being seen.[96]

Americans know that their public appearances are subject to video recording through closed circuit cameras, mobile phones, and other such devices carried by people in public who are filming their own activities. Most surveillance devices are used by

---

[94] Ibid.,71.

[95] Anne Brunon-Ernst, *Beyond Foucault: New Perspectives On Bentham's Panopticon* (Burlington, VT: Ashgate, 2012), xi.

[96] Michel Foucault, *Discipline and Punish: The Birth of the Prison* (New York: Pantheon Books, 1977), 201–2.

landowners and employers for security purposes to avoid claims of negligence.[97] Even with the myriad recording devices used in public, people still retain a bit of anonymity and can feel relatively sure that, for the most part, the surveillance to which they are being subjected is not active surveillance in the sense that panopticism is not taking place. Facial recognition technology like the Department of Homeland Security's BOSS, however, degrades privacy by identifying individuals instantly and removing the privacy of anonymity. The government uses facial recognition technology to increase security through surveillance, but employing FRT may actually increase *insecurity* through societal transformation.[98]

Using FRT and active surveillance for a comprehensive documentation of peoples' locations and activities is a violation of privacy as described by Westin and Fried in Gormley's third and fourth privacy clusters. Donald Zoufal wrote in his 2008 master's thesis, "Someone to Watch over Me? Privacy and Governance Strategies for CCTV and Emerging Surveillance Technologies":

> With the advent of digitization technology, that allows for the cataloguing and compiling of massive amounts of data, it is this documentation feature of the Panopticon that can dramatically shift power between the individual and his or her government. The ultimate effect of this compilation of data that allows the subsequent manipulation of the individual is not known. However, the dramatic shift in power between the individual and government needs to be recognized.[99]

Indeed, society must recognize the power afforded to the government by the employment of active facial recognition surveillance and congress must pass legislation to appropriately govern future surveillance technologies. The outlook for panopticism is not entirely negative. Strictly speaking, the Panopticon was a structural design allowing

---

[97] Robert D. Bickel, Susan Brinkley, and Wendy White, "Seeing Past Privacy: Will the Development and Application of CCTV and Other Video Security Technology Compromise an Essential Constitutional Right in a Democracy, or Will the Courts Strike a Proper Balance?," *Stetson Law Review* 33, no. 1 (2003), http://www.stetson.edu/law/lawreview/media/seeing-past-privacy-will-the-development-and-application-of-cctv-and-other-video-security-technology-compromise-an-essential-constitutional-right-in-a-democracy-or-will-the-courts-strike-a-proper-ba.pdf.

[98] Mitchell Gray, "Urban Surveillance and Panopticism: Will We Recognize the Facial Recognition Society?," Surveillance and Society 1 (3) (2003), 314–330, http://www.surveillance-and-society.org/articles1%283%29/facial.pdf.

[99] Zoufal, "Someone to Watch," 45.

total observation and documentation. However, there are features of the Panopticon that allow the watchers to oversee and regulate to without interrupting the operations of the Panopticon. For instance, Foucault points out:

> The arrangement of this machine is such that its enclosed nature does not preclude a permanent presence from the outside: we have seen that anyone may come and exercise in the central tower the functions of surveillance, and…he can gain a clear idea of the way in which the surveillance is being practiced. In fact, any panoptic institution…may without difficulty be subjected to such irregular and constant inspections: and not only by the appointed inspectors, but also by the public…The seeing machine was once a sort of dark room into which individuals spied; it has become a transparent building in which the exercise of power may be supervised by society as a whole.[100]

Using panopticism example, the public can be protected from abuse and overreaching by government surveillance through frequent and unannounced inspections and openness in surveillance programs. Transparency allows for the public and inspectors to ensure that government agencies are properly observing the public's wishes, applying requisite laws and policies, and maintaining the appropriate level of privacy.

2.   Surveillance and Behavior

Surveillance seeks to solve security problems through preemption, but brings with it a new set of problems to consider. Coupling facial recognition and surveillance calls for new laws to protect privacy. As Senator Franken noted at a 2012 Senate hearing titled *What Facial Recognition Technology Means for Privacy and Civil Liberties,* a concern exists among Americans that surveillance aided by facial recognition technology may, "eventually come at a very high cost to our civil liberties."[101] He then introduces the concerns of law:

> Unlike what we have in place for wiretaps and other surveillance devices, there is no law regulating law enforcement use of facial recognition

---

[100] Foucault, *Discipline and Punish*, 207.

[101] Al Franken, Senator, United States Senate, Committee on the Judiciary, Subcommittee on Privacy, Technology and the Law, *What Facial Recognition Technology Means for Privacy and Civil Liberties: Hearing Before the Subcommittee On Privacy, Technology and the Law of the Committee On the Judiciary, United States Senate, One Hundred Twelfth Congress, Second Session, July 18, 2012* (Washington: U.S. Government Printing Office, 2012).

technology. And current Fourth Amendment case law generally says that we have no reasonable expectation of privacy in what we voluntarily expose to the public—yet we can hardly leave our houses in the morning without exposing our faces to the public. So law enforcement doesn't need a warrant to use this technology on someone. It might not even need to have a reasonable suspicion that the subject has been involved in a crime.[102]

One solution to Senator Franken's concerns about unknowingly participating in active surveillance is posting signs everywhere that inform potential participants that facial recognition technology is in use. Similar to the "Smile. You're on camera" signs that retail shops popularly post in the United States, FRT warning signs would serve to create panopticism and modify the behavior of the people who read the signs. When people under surveillance in a democratic society are not aware of the surveillance, there is no transparency in their democracy and they run a risk of developing totalitarianism, or at least run the risk of privacy-demeaning mission creep.

There are panoptic effects of people who know they are under surveillance in public. The resulting social control is dangerous and compounds with advanced technology. Jeffrey Reiman writes about this phenomenon:

> When you know you are being observed, you naturally identify with the outside observer's viewpoint, and add that alongside your own viewpoint on your action. This double vision makes your act different, whether the act is making love or taking a drive. The targets of the panopticon know and feel the eye of the guard on them, making their actions different than if they were done in private. Their repertoire of possible actions diminishes as they lose those choices whose intrinsic nature depends on privacy.[103]

Reiman's "double vision" is more likely when a subject knows their actions are being recorded. Richard Wasserstrom notes that people who know data is being collected on them measure their actions more carefully:

[102] Franken, *What Facial Recognition Technology Means.*

[103] Jeffrey H. Reiman, "Driving to the Panopticon: A Philosophical Exploration of the Risks to Privacy Posed by the Highway Technology of the Future," *Santa Clara Computer and High Technology Law Journal* 11, no. 1 (1995), http://digitalcommons.law.scu.edu/chtlj/vol11/iss1/5.

No matter how innocent one's intentions and actions at any given moment, I think that an inevitable consequence of such a practice of data collection would be that persons would think more carefully before they did things that would become part of the record. Life would to this degree become less spontaneous and more measured.[104]

Public surveillance is a fantastic tool for security and investigations, but in a free and open society, it is a hindrance to ordinary behavior. A society that promotes freedom of action should not employ devices that alter people's behavior. As Christopher Slobogin notes:

People who know they are under government surveillance will act less spontaneously, more deliberately, less individualistically, and more conventionally; conduct on the streets that is outside the mainstream, susceptible to suspicious interpretation, or merely conspicuous…will diminish and perhaps even be officially squelched.[105]

A free society must allow its people to act freely and possess the feeling of security provided by remaining anonymous in public. When people feel like the authorities are constantly identifying and monitoring their actions in public, panoptic effects abound and social control thrives.

---

[104] Richard A. Wasserstrom, "Privacy: Some Arguments and Assumptions," in *Philosophical Dimensions of Privacy: An Anthology,* ed. Ferdinand D. Schoeman (Cambridge: Cambridge University Press, 1984), 328.

[105] Christopher Slobogin, "Public Privacy: Camera Surveillance of Public Places and the Right to Anonymity," *Mississippi Law Journal* 72, no. 1 (2002), http://dx.doi.org/10.2139/ssrn.364600.

THIS PAGE INTENTIONALLY LEFT BLANK

IV. PRIVACY, SURVEILLANCE, AND THE FOURTH AMENDMENT

There is no constitutional protection against unregulated, omnipresent monitoring of the public by government security agencies. When asked about the CIA's responsibilities to privacy and civil liberties, General Michael Hayden, the Director of the CIA at the time, who often liked to use sports analogies, famously quipped that when it came to civil liberties and intelligence tasks, he would always stay in fair territory, but it was his duty to play right up to the line. Specifically, he said, he would play fair, but there would be chalk dust on his cleats.[106] In other words, it is the responsibility of government security agencies to push the envelope of civil liberties using every effort to provide security.

Facial recognition technology pushes the privacy envelope and the implementation of active identification through surveillance using FRT is a development in the privacy-versus-security debate that society should explore. It is the responsibility of lawmakers to pass legislation to protect civil liberties and keep the "chalk line" in an appropriate location to allow government security agencies and police to conduct efficient surveillance and still protect Americans' privacy expectations under the law.

In 1890, in the Harvard Law Review, Warren and Brandeis announced two important points regarding personal privacy.[107] The first was that times were changing and the rules associated with defining and protecting privacy must take societal (and technological) changes into consideration. The second was that the "right to be let alone," as Judge Cooley paraphrased it, extended to people even outside of their home.[108] The article is closely associated with the 1928 *Olmstead* decision and the 1967 *Katz* decision. From these writings and early court cases, we can see how Americans are developing their expectations of privacy.

---

[106] Michael V. Hayden, "CIA Director's Address at Duquesne University Commencement," Central Intelligence Agency, May 4, 2007, https://www.cia.gov/news-information/speeches-testimony/2007/cia-directors-address-at-duquesne-university-commencement.html.

[107] Warren and Brandeis, "The Right to Privacy."

[108] Ibid.

At the heart of most privacy cases is the distinction between what societies consider private and what they consider public.[109] Historically speaking, ancient biblical texts and Greek and Roman law were the underpinnings of the Fourth Amendment to the United States Constitution—where a man's home was his castle.[110] There is a strong foundation in U.S. case law that establishes the home as the center of privacy, and no one, including agents of the government, may violate that privacy without a reasonable cause. The issue with facial recognition technology does not currently affect privacy in the home, so one must look farther from the home to determine if FRT violates privacy expectations.

The Fourth Amendment protects people and their possessions against unreasonable searches and seizures.[111] The use of facial recognition technology by police and government security agencies is not a violation of privacy guarantees under the Fourth Amendment. Rather, a limited right to privacy has been established by the United States Supreme Court as a "penumbral right," a right guaranteed through implication, in a series of cases that this chapter will examine.[112] This chapter will explore relevant legislation and jurisprudence on the issues of privacy, surveillance, technology, and applications of the law relating to facial recognition surveillance.

A.   EARLY COURT INTERPRETATIONS

The early traditional method of determining whether a given search violated the Fourth Amendment relied on the tort of trespass. This method of determining a search violation hails from the time when the nation first adopted the Fourth Amendment. The violation occurred with "a physical intrusion on private property."[113] Many cases since

---

[109] Turkington, "Privacy Law," 2.

[110] Nelson Lasson, "The History and Development of the Fourth Amendment to the United States Constitution," in *Privacy Law: Cases and Materials,* by Richard C. Turkington and Anita L. Allen (St. Paul, MN: West Group, 2002) 7–8.

[111] U.S. Const., amend. IV.

[112] Turkington, "Privacy Law," 63.

[113] Brown, "Anonymity," 11.

the late 19ᵗʰ century have found this literal interpretation of the Fourth Amendment to be out of date and not in keeping with the spirit of the Constitutional framers' intent regarding protection against unreasonable search and seizure.

Supreme Court decisions often cite *Boyd v. United States*[114] as a landmark case that demonstrated no physical intrusion need have occurred to violate protection against unreasonable search and seizure as protected by the Fourth Amendment. In *Boyd,* the court found that the government could not compel a defendant to produce papers that would incriminate him in court. While this case touches on the Fifth Amendment's protection against self-incrimination, the signal holding relates to the Fourth Amendment.[115] Kimberly Brown wrote that the framers of the Constitution were aware of the "arbitrary powers" the government could possess, and it was against this danger that they were guarding when they wrote the Fourth and Fifth Amendments:

> In refusing to uphold a court order directing a defendant in a civil forfeiture proceeding to produce documentary evidence of liability, the court framed the "essence" of the government's offense as "the invasion of the indefeasible right of personal security, personal liberty and private property," as the framers were keenly attuned to "the struggles against arbitrary power in which they had been engaged for more than 20 years" when they approved the Fourth and Fifth Amendments.[116]

In *Olmstead v. United States,*[117] the majority based its decision on the fact that a physical intrusion had not occurred, and therefore the government had not violated the Fourth Amendment:

> Neither the cases we have cited nor any of the many federal decisions brought to our attention hold the Fourth Amendment to have been violated as against a defendant unless there has been an official search and seizure of his person, or such a seizure of his papers or his tangible material effects, or an actual physical invasion of his house "or curtilage" for the purpose of making a seizure.[118]

---

[114] Boyd v. United States, 116 U.S. 616 (1886).

[115] U.S. Const., amend. V.

[116] Brown, "Anonymity," 12.

[117] Olmstead v. United States, 277 U.S. 438 (1928).

[118] Ibid.

The *Olmstead* opinion was based on the original tort laws against trespass. Louis Brandeis famously dissented from the majority's judgment in *Olmstead* by claiming that wiretapping *did* violate the Fourth Amendment even though a physical trespass had not occurred and he cited *Boyd*, among others, to prove the violation. The advancement of technology had allowed the government to intrude on the essence of a man's privacy expectations in a way that the framers of the Constitution could not have imagined:

> The makers of our Constitution…knew that only a part of the pain, pleasure, and satisfactions of life are to be found in material things. They sought to protect Americans in their beliefs, their thoughts, their emotions, and their sensations. They conferred, as against the Government, the right to be let alone—the most comprehensive of rights and the right most valued by civilized men. To protect that right, every unjustifiable intrusion by the Government upon the privacy of the individual, whatever the means employed, must be deemed a violation of the Fourth Amendment.[119]

In the *Katz* decision, Justice Harlan concurred with the majority opinion of the court that electronic eavesdropping requires a warrant, but he qualified his opinion in what several more recent court cases refer to as the Harlan elaboration.[120] In it, Justice Harlan explains that the *Katz* decision protects *people* and not *places*. Therefore, the case established that even outside the home, people have some expectation of privacy. Additionally, the Harlan elaboration noted that in order for a breach of privacy to occur, the situation must pass a two-part test; namely, "a person [must] have exhibited an actual (subjective) expectation of privacy,"[121] and, "the expectation [must] be one that society is prepared to recognize as 'reasonable.'"[122]

When relating the Harlan elaboration to facial recognition technology, one can observe that people in public fail the first part of the two-part test. That is, they do not exhibit an actual subjective expectation of privacy. People displaying their faces in public are, in effect, declaring that they are prepared to accept that others will see their faces and

---

[119] Olmstead v. United States, 277 U.S. 438 (1928).

[120] La Fave, *Search and Seizure*, 579.

[121] Ibid.

[122] Ibid.

therefore they are not demonstrating a desire for privacy, at least to the image of their face.

Justice Harlan's first test, demonstrating a subjective expectation of privacy, is easy for government agencies to overcome; the courts should not consider it a hard-and-fast rule. La Fave demonstrates why:

> An actual, subjective expectation of privacy obviously has no place in a statement of what *Katz* held or in theory of what the Fourth Amendment protects. It can neither add to, nor can its absence detract from, an individual's claim to Fourth Amendment protection. If it could, the government could diminish each person's subjective expectation of privacy merely by announcing half-hourly on television that we were all forthwith being placed under comprehensive electronic surveillance.[123]

The New York Law Review in 1968 referred to the *Katz* decision as a "watershed" moment in Fourth Amendment jurisprudence because, "the court purported to clean house on outmoded fourth amendment principles."[124] Government electronic surveillance no longer needed to pass the trespass or property-based test. Instead, in *Katz,* the court found that Brandeis' "right to be let alone" was the test for Fourth Amendment privacy protections and various courts have repeated this decision many times since *Katz.*[125]

Although *Katz* represented a turning point in privacy jurisprudence, the decision did not provide privacy protection for technology like FRT. The *Katz* decision noted that "what a person knowingly exposes to the public, even in his own home or office, is not a subject of Fourth Amendment protection."[126] Further, in *New York v. Class,*[127] the court found that since "the exterior of a car...is thrust into the public eye...to examine it does not constitute a search."[128] The court also found that there is no reasonable expectation of

---

[123] La Fave, *Search and Seizure*, 583.

[124] Ibid., 580.

[125] Brown, "Anonymity," 12.

[126] Katz v. United States, 389 U.S. 347 (1967).

[127] New York v. Class, 475 U.S. 106 (1986).

[128] Ibid.

privacy associated with the movements of a person travelling in a vehicle on public thoroughfares.[129]

A reasonable conclusion to draw from these pre-digital–age legal decisions is that the courts have shown that a person knowingly exposing their face in public and, while moving about in the public eye, has no reasonable expectation of privacy when it comes to their faceprint being collected and used to identify them. The courts have held that "mere visual observation does not constitute a search."[130]

Douglas A. Fretty, a corporate lawyer in California, points out that the argument in favor of government surveillance is strong, "that where people lack an expectation of not being observed, they equally lack an expectation of not being recognized."[131] Put another way, if people know they may be observed in public, then they can reasonably expect they may be identified. Kimberly Brown writes that face scanning in public is no different than the visual observation society expects of a police officer in the regular course of his duties on patrol:

> To the extent that FRT is considered part and parcel of the traditional visual surveillance that police conduct in unmarked vehicles—which has long been considered constitutional—the Fourth Amendment does not apply. FRT also targets an area of the body that a person would not reasonably expect to consider private.[132]

Justice Scalia, in his dissenting opinion in *Maryland v. King*[133] quoted *Katz* and proclaimed that "we have never held that merely taking a person's photograph invades any recognized 'expectation of privacy.'"[134] In addition to the lawful taking of a photograph, the courts have recognized that identifying a person is also in line with the

---

[129] United States v. Knotts, 460 U.S. 276 (1983).

[130] United States v. Jones, 132 S.Ct. 945 (2012).

[131] Douglas A. Fretty, "Face-Recognition Surveillance: A Moment of Truth for Fourth Amendment Rights in Public Places," *Virginia Journal of Law & Technology* 16, no. 3 (2011). http://www.vjolt.net/ vol16/issue3/v16i3_430-Fretty.pdf.

[132] Brown, "Anonymity," 12.

[133] Maryland v. King, 133 S.Ct. 1958, (2013).

[134] Ibid.

constitution. This finding is evident in *Hiibel v. Sixth Judicial District Court*[135] where the Supreme Court upheld the Nevada state law that required people to identify themselves to police officers upon request, even when the identification was not in the line of investigating a crime. This case is especially important when considering the advancement of technology in the future because Justice Stevens' dissenting opinion notes that the ability to attach a name to "a broad array of information about the person … can be tremendously useful in a criminal prosecution."[136]

B. SURVEILLANCE LEGALITY

When faced with the question of FRT surveillance legality, advocates for the practice point to common traditions of police identification. For example, Dennis Bailey compares FRT surveillance to police identification through a mug-shot database:

> The great thing about a facial-recognition system is that a human being can verify the results. After a hit is made, a security officer can take the flagged individual aside and do a careful comparison with the picture in the database. This is no different from when a police officer pulls over a suspect and compares his or her face to the image on a printed copy of a mug shot.[137]

John Woodward writes that facial recognition is a common technique used every day and is of no real concern. "One could argue that 'facial recognition' is a standard identification technique and that it raises no special concerns. After all, we look at each other's faces to recognize one another. Police regularly use mug shots to identify criminals. And we think nothing of being asked to display 'photo ID' to confirm our identity."[138]

While Bailey's and Woodward's examples of common tactics for identification are technically correct, these tactics require a significantly longer time to make an

---

[135] Hiibel v. Sixth Judicial District Court, 542 U.S. 177 (2004).

[136] Hiibel v. Sixth Judicial District Court, 542 U.S. 177 (2004).

[137] Dennis Bailey, *The Open Society Paradox: Why the 21st Century Calls for More Openness—Not Less* (Dulles, VA: Potomac, 2004), 92.

[138] Woodward, John D. Jr. and Arroyo Center, *Super Bowl Surveillance: Facing Up to Biometrics* (Santa Monica, CA: RAND Arroyo Center, 2001), 3.

identification than FRT surveillance. Julie Petersen writes that the speed with which police can search mug shot databases is increasing as the technology develops:

> Law enforcement agencies…use many visual matching tools with online databanks, systems that are gradually superseding paper files, and books full of mug shots. Search and retrieval systems for accessing and sorting information stored in databases are becoming faster and more powerful.[139]

Taking into account the advancement of technology, and the historically common techniques police use for identification, one might argue that FRT is simply a faster way of looking through a mug shot book.

What Bailey and Woodward do not address in their examples is the potential for FRT, employed in a public place for surveillance, to capture the images of innocent people without their knowledge that are later potentially compared to a criminal database. Jennifer Lynch, of the Electronic Frontier Foundation, is a leading expert in facial recognition who has testified before Congress on the implications of government and private development of FRT. She writes:

> Some have…suggested the false-positive risk inherent in large facial recognition databases could result in…[altering] the traditional presumption of innocence in criminal cases by placing more of a burden on the defendant to show he is *not* who the system identifies him to be. And this is true even if a face recognition system such as NGI offers several results for a search instead of one, because each of the people identified could be brought in for questioning, even if he…was not involved in the crime. In light of this, German Federal Data Protection Commissioner Peter Schaar has noted that false positives in facial recognition systems pose a large problem for democratic societies: "in the event of a genuine hunt, [they] render innocent people suspects for a time, create a need for justification on their part, and make further checks by the authorities unavoidable."[140]

Even in the event that the government finds innocent people identified through surveillance, the relevant jurisprudence suggests that the situation is not a problem. In

---

[139] Julie K. Petersen, *Understanding Surveillance Technologies: Spy Devices, Privacy, History & Applications* (Boca Raton: Auerbach Publications, 2007), 483.

[140] Jennifer Lynch, "What Facial Recognition Technology Means for Privacy and Civil Liberties," Written Testimony of Jennifer Lynch, Staff Attorney with the Electronic Frontier Foundation (EFF), Senate Committee on the Judiciary, Subcommittee on Privacy, Technology, and the Law, July 18, 2012, https://www.eff.org/files/filenode/jenniferlynch_eff-senate-testimony-face_recognition.pdf.

United States v. Mara,[141] the court found that a grand jury can compel a person to supply writing or speech samples for comparison in an investigation, even if the person is not a suspect, because people commonly display those things in public. Similarly, in *United States v. Dionisio,*[142] the court stated that "no person can have a reasonable expectation that others will not know the sound of his voice, any more than he can reasonably expect that his face will be a mystery to the world."[143] While the courts did not examine these cases under the circumstances of a surveillance state, they demonstrated the courts' position on the privacy, or lack thereof, of a person's face in public.[144]

Courts have also found, however, that people expect "not to be identified in public by sophisticated algorithms."[145] In *Lopez v. United States*[146] the court specifically warned against new technology (in this case, a personal audio recording device) and the impact to privacy expectations: "the fantastic advances in the field of electronic communication constitute a great danger to the privacy of the individual; that indiscriminate use of such devices in law enforcement raises grave constitutional questions."[147]

There is evidence that the American public in general does not approve of FRT surveillance. As discussed in the Introduction to this thesis, the Ybor City experiment not only showed that FRT was not technically ready for employment, but it showed that on a large scale, people did not want to be arbitrarily identified in public. At Super Bowl XXXV, in February 2002, police used FRT surveillance in order to identify criminals entering the event. The practice of employing FRT drew significant criticism, especially from the American Civil Liberties Union (ACLU). Although it was only five

---

[141] United States v. Mara, 410 U.S. 19 (1973).

[142] United States v. Dionisio, 410 U.S. 1 (1973).

[143] Ibid.

[144] Fretty, "Face-Recognition," 18.

[145] Ibid.

[146] Lopez v. United States, 373 U.S. 427 (1963).

[147] Ibid.

months since the terrorist attacks of 9/11, "the use of FRT at the Super Bowl was overwhelmingly negative."[148] The ACLU acted quickly:

> The response from privacy advocates was fast, furious, and predictable: The ACLU condemned the Super Bowl system…as the Snooper Bowl and asked the mayor and city council of Tampa, Fla. To hold public hearings on the topic. The ACLU argued that the public did not agree to be subjected to a computerized police lineup as a condition of admission.[149]

The courts could interpret public outrage at privacy violations using FRT surveillance as inconsequential. In *Dow Chemical Co. v. United States,*[150] the court determined that when technology is commonly available for public use, and the police only use it to enhance their natural abilities (not to see through walls or hear normally imperceptible conversations), the surveillance is constitutionally permitted.[151] The courts have raised questions of whether FRT is a technology commonly available to the public and they have determined it is. Fretty writes that online programs such as Polar Rose and Google Profile are commonly available: "Members of the public could conceivably use an online FRT program such as Polar Rose to identify strangers on the street based on a furtively-snapped digital photo. Google is now building an application that would locate a person's online Google Profile based on any photo of the person's face."[152]

It appears the courts will continue to battle with the question of privacy expectations for individual identifications made using active surveillance. Justice Kozinski writes in his dissent in *United States v. Pineda-Moreno,*[153] a phrase that, for its modernity and relevance to technology and privacy, may become a well-known and often cited reaction to FRT surveillance: "There is something creepy and un-American about such clandestine and underhanded [continuous surveillance]…We are taking a giant leap into the unknown, and the consequences for ourselves and our children may be dire and

---

[148] Fretty, "Face-Recognition," 19.

[149] Glee Harrah Cady and Pat McGregor, *Protect Your Digital Privacy: Survival Skills for the Information Age* (Indianapolis: Que, 2002), 173–4.

[150] Dow Chemical Co. v. United States, 476 U.S. 227 (1986).

[151] Fretty, "Face-Recognition," 16–7.

[152] Ibid., 19.

[153] United States v. Pineda-Moreno, 591 F.3d 1212 (9th Cir. 2010).

irreversible. Some day, soon, we may wake up and find we're living in [Orwell's] Oceania."[154]

C.   NEW TECHNOLOGICAL AGE

Courts and legislators have contended with the issue of the government's use of advancing technology and its effects on privacy security.[155] In *Olmstead,* Justice Taft delivered the opinion of the court and noted that while there was not wording in the Fourth Amendment that provided protection against wiretaps, "discovery and invention have made it possible for the Government...to obtain disclosure in court of what is whispered in the closet."[156] Justice Taft also noted that a person inside their home, a privacy-protected area, who utters words over a line that projects the words to the outside of the home, expects those words to remain private, and Congress should pass direct legislation to protect them. Congress accommodated the courts in 1934, with the passage of the Federal Communications Act. Electronic surveillance was addressed in § 605, which stated that electronic communications were to be protected as private to the sender and recipient.[157]

In 1968, in response to the limited protections of the Electronic Surveillance Act, Congress passed the Omnibus Crime Control and Safe Streets Act of 1968. Title III of the act regulated, "virtually all forms of electronic surveillance of conversations."[158] The Act sought to accommodate law enforcement in using new technology to combat crime, but also temper law enforcement efforts in a way that accommodated citizens' reasonable privacy expectations.

By 1986, Congress had amended Title III by enacting the Electronic Communications Privacy Act of 1986. The intent of this amendment was to update Title III to clarify legislation for advancements in technology. Title III originally included only

---

[154] Ibid.

[155] Brown, "Anonymity," 13.

[156] Olmstead v. United States, 277 U.S. 438 (1928).

[157] Turkington, *Privacy Law,* 294.

[158] Ibid., 295.

analog conversations, but the amendment governed, "the surveillance of digitally transmitted conversations, electronic mail, cellular phones, and pen registers."[159]

Despite the positive advancements made in legislation to protect privacy in the digital age while still allowing the government to conduct effective investigations, the courts continually face cases that challenge the constitutionality of developments in privacy-challenging technology.

The court found, in 1983, that the use of technology to aide in searching, in this case a flashlight, did not violate the expectation of privacy when used for illuminating the interior of a car during a traffic stop.[160] Additionally, in *California v. Ciraolo,*[161] the court found that plain-view observation from an aircraft was not violative of Fourth Amendment privacy protections because any member of the public who was flying that day could have witnessed what the police saw, Ciraolo's marijuana cultivation in the back yard.[162]

More recently, *Kyllo,* discussed in Chapter I, has become the landmark case concerning the use of emerging technology to aid in searches. Justice Alito commented in *Florida v. Jardines,*[163] that *Kyllo* was a "decision about the use of new technology."[164] Justice Scalia, who wrote for the majority in *Jardines,* observed that *Kyllo* was "a case involving surveillance technology that allows law enforcement to learn details 'that would previously have been unknowable without physical intrusion.'"[165]

The court also grappled with the place of technology, in relation to the Fourth Amendment and privacy, in *United States v. Jones.*[166] There, the court found that when police placed a GPS device on the defendant's vehicle for the purpose of tracking his

---

[159] Ibid., 296.

[160] Texas v. Brown, 460 U.S. 730 (1983).

[161] California v. Ciraolo, 476 U.S. 207 (1986).

[162] Ibid.

[163] Florida v. Jardines, 133 S.Ct. 1409 (2013).

[164] Ibid.

[165] Brown, "Anonymity," 13.

[166] United States v. Jones, 132 S.Ct. 945 (2012).

movements, the move was violative of the Fourth Amendment because, police violated the trespass test when they placed the device. Some key reasoning came out of the case, however, because although Justice Scalia used the trespass test to judge the case, Justice Alito stated:

> Because GPS technology was relatively easy and cheap, it overcomes traditional practical constraints on close surveillance and…its use violated society's expectation that law enforcement would and could not monitor all of an individual's movements in his car for a 4-week period. While relatively short-term monitoring of an individual's movements on public streets may be reasonable, "the use of longer term GPS monitoring in investigations of most offenses impinges on expectations of privacy."[167]

Justice Alito's last point comes from "mosaic theory," which reasons the whole of surveillance activity is greater than the sum of its parts.[168] Mosaic theory supposes that "the sequence of a person's movements may reveal more than the individual movements of which it is composed."[169] When employing FRT surveillance—and considering the aggregation of information available about a person from the FBI's NGI, or various open-source information people post about themselves on the Internet, or information available from private companies—the government could establish a very nearly complete picture of the personal information and activities of unsuspecting people moving around in public.

It appears the court is coming closer to determining the place for surveillance technology in privacy. The decision from *Knotts* in 1983, demonstrated that people can have no reasonable expectation of privacy in their movements on public streets, but it did not address the place of technology in that determination. *Jones* in 2012, however, considered the place of GPS tracking technology and the aggregation of information described by the mosaic theory. Kimberly Brown notes that Justices Sotomayor, Alito, Ginsberg, Breyer, and Kagan have all recently "expressed concern that modern

---

[167] United States v. Jones, Case Brief Summary, last modified November 30, 2013, http://www.casebriefsummary.com/united-states-v-jones/.

[168] Richard M. Thompson II, "*United States v. Jones:* GPS Monitoring, Property, and Privacy," Congressional Research Service, April 30, 2012, 7.

[169] United States v. Maynard, 615 F.3d 544, 558 (D.C. Cir. 2010).

technology is eroding individuals' ability to be free of government monitoring."[170] She quotes Justice Sotomayor's concern:

> Electronic or other novel modes of surveillance can generate a precise, comprehensive record of a person's public movements that reflects a wealth of detail about her familial, political, professional, religious, and sexual associations—without any physical invasion of property. The government…can store and mine such data indefinitely. Because modern electronic surveillance is cheap by comparison to traditional surveillance techniques, it "proceeds surreptitiously" and "evades the ordinary checks that constrain abusive law enforcement practices: "limited police resources and community hostility."[171]

Although current laws in the United States do not prevent the government from employing technology like FRT surveillance, the courts are steadily moving toward a position that considers the place of technology in the realm of privacy expectations relating to the Fourth Amendment. Given the jurisprudence established by past courts, the privacy expectations of people in their activities and anonymity in public, and the advancement of technology that facilitates a mosaic of private information within seconds of searching, Congress should pass early legislation regulating the employment of FRT surveillance in the public.

---

[170] Brown, "Anonymity," 14.

[171] Brown, "Anonymity," 14.

V.   CONCLUSION

This thesis has shown that facial recognition technology holds great opportunities for policing and government security by making mass surveillance more efficient. In mass surveillance, however, privacy pays the cost for surveillance efficiency.

FRT has developed substantially in the past few decades, but it has had limited success in practical applications. By using advancing technology, researchers are quickly overcoming traditional technical problems they faced in the past. Research in the field of infrared imagery and three-dimensional image captures is advancing at a rapid pace and the commercial and security demand for FRT is growing.[172] The advancement of FRT means that government and private security can identify people in public at a rate much more rapidly than traditional methods required.

A sense of anonymity is important to people as they move about in public and interact within their community. The knowledge of active surveillance changes how people behave and can lead to moderately controlling behavior because people act differently when they know authorities are watching. In the same way that a stationary police car sitting overtly on the side of the interstate causes traffic to slow within eyeshot of the vehicle, overt surveillance, especially with the possibility of recognition, can serve to modify behavior on a massive scale.[173] The perceived risk of apprehension modifies motorists' behavior when they are within sight of the enforcer.[174]

While the police are only modifying behavior in a small area while enforcing traffic laws, behavior modification on a large scale is a form of social control. People who know that authorities are watching them modify their behavior. This type of behavior modification is how prisons successfully employ the Panopticon to help ensure prisoners' compliance to the rules. Even if the guards are not monitoring a prisoner, the

---

[172] Seong G. Kong, "Recent Advances in Visual and Infrared Face Recognition—A Review," *Computer Vision and Image Understanding* 97, no. 1 (2005): 103–35, doi:10.1016/j.cviu.2004.04.001.

[173] David Shinar and A. James McKnight, "The Effects of Enforcement and Public Information on Compliance," *Human Behavior and Traffic Safety* (1985): 385–419, doi:10.1007/978-1-4613-2173-6_17.

[174] Ibid.

prisoner has the illusion and sense of constant monitoring and thus their behaviors are modified so they conform to the rules.

A.   LEGAL ANALYSIS

Early interpretations of the Fourth Amendment have shown that the trespass test is no longer the sole means of identifying a breach of constitutionally protected privacy expectations. The courts have shown the important ability to reason with changing times and embracing technological change. The courts no longer take the words of the Fourth Amendment literally, but the spirit of the Amendment is what they debate. By employing the spirit of the Amendment, the courts have shown that privacy is connected to people, not places, and that a person should have no expectation of privacy in the things they thrust into the public eye. But what a person thrusts into the public eye is no longer just an anonymous face on the street. The advancement of technology has made a person's face the passport to their identity.

As noted in Chapter II, public identification and logging location data of individuals as they move about in public should be principally disturbing to people for whom the police have no particular reason for watching. Is identifying a person's personal information, without a warrant, through public FRT surveillance, a violation of Fourth Amendment protections against unreasonable search and seizure? This thesis has shown that it is not a violation, but that the courts are on the verge of a breakthrough for deciding whether privacy or security should weigh more heavily in the realm of advancing technology. Doug Fretty sums up the place of FRT in the privacy-versus-security debate in his short conclusion:

> As innovations in digital surveillance have accelerated, fundamental uncertainties have emerged in Fourth Amendment jurisprudence. The fault lines of contemporary search-and-seizure law expose such questions as: whether we enjoy a reasonable expectation of anonymity in public, whether a person can be virtually "seized" by sophisticated technology that does not impede movement, and whether people truly cede privacy expectations in data revealed to ISPs. Face-recognition surveillance necessarily confronts each of these questions and more head-on, and, as a result, a constitutional challenge to this new technique may serve as a harbinger for the Fourth Amendment's ambit in the digital era. Courts will

use the opportunity either to shore up the "right of the people to be secure," or to admit how little the Amendment safeguards once we emerge from our homes.[175]

People displaying their faces in public and moving about in public places can have no reasonable expectation of privacy according to early privacy jurisprudence, and current legislation and the Fourth Amendment do not expressly prohibit FRT-style surveillance as interpreted by the courts. However, the courts have shown a propensity to mature with technology and they are likely to decide soon whether or not people should have a right to keep their identity private in public places.

B.   FUTURE RESEARCH

Future research in this area could combine First Amendment protections for anonymity with Fourth Amendment principles in the field of advancing technology to protect privacy and anonymity where FRT is employed. As publicly available data is widely collected by both private and public entities, massive searchable databases are available to identify patterns that are not available in a single source.[176] Future research can identify jurisprudence for lawmakers to consider when drafting legislation for outdated privacy protection laws.

C.   REFLECTIONS

This thesis sought to answer whether facial recognition surveillance violates Fourth Amendment privacy protections and to what extent, and whether law enforcement and government security professionals can use facial recognition surveillance for combatting crime while continuing to protect the public's privacy expectations. The advancement of FRT technology was compared to the relevant topics and jurisprudence relating to privacy and it was determined that a person cannot assume their identity is protected when they show their face in public.

Some 125 years ago, Warren and Brandeis pointed out that times are changing with evolving technology and society must be prepared to write and accept laws that

---

[175] Fretty, "Face-Recognition," 45–6.

[176] Brown, "Anonymity," 22.

53

account for societal and technological changes. Proper early legislation should precede massive employment of facial recognition technology, so Americans can explore the level of acceptable privacy manipulations they are willing to tolerate in exchange for security.

Westin wrote that in order for people to accept unreasonableness for the purpose of greater security, the "very real and presently rising risk of jeopardizing the public's confidence in its daily freedoms from unreasonable invasions of privacy,"[177] must be serious enough to allow it. If the security enjoyed by our society is at such a risk that we are willing to unreasonably trade our privacy, we may also be trading our liberty—for when anonymity is destroyed, and the Panopticon is built, our behaviors are modified and social control is the result. As Justice Kozinski stated, continuous government surveillance is "creepy and un-American."[178] In order to maintain the values of privacy Americans expect, appropriate legislation is required. That legislation is on the horizon, but until then, privacy will lose in the face of surveillance.

---

[177] Westin, *Privacy and Freedom*, 370.

[178] United States v. Pineda-Moreno, 591 F.3d 1212 (9th Cir. 2010).

LIST OF REFERENCES

Arendt, Hannah. *The Human Condition.* Chicago: University of Chicago Press, 1958.

Bailey, Dennis. *The Open Society Paradox: Why the 21ˢᵗ Century Calls for More Openness—Not Less.* Dulles, VA: Potomac, 2004.

Brunon-Ernst, Anne. *Beyond Foucault: New Perspectives On Bentham's Panopticon,* Burlington, VT: Ashgate, 2012.

Cady, Glee Harrah and Pat McGregor. *Protect Your Digital Privacy: Survival Skills for the Information Age.* Indianapolis: Que, 2002.

Cate, Fred H. *Privacy in the Information Age.* Washington, D.C.: Brookings Institution Press, 1997.

Coleman, Roy and Michael McCahill. *Surveillance and Crime.* Thousand Oaks, CA: Sage Publications, 2011.

Friedrich, Carl J. "Secrecy versus Privacy: The Democratic Dilemma." In *Privacy,* edited by J. Roland Pennock and John W. Chapman, 105–20. New York: Atherton Press, 1971.

Foucault, Michel. *Discipline and Punish: The Birth of the Prison.* New York: Pantheon Books, 1977.

Gates, Kelly A. *Our Biometric Future: Facial Recognition Technology and the Culture of Surveillance.* New York: New York University Press, 2011.

Herman, Susan N. *Taking Liberties: The War on Terror and the Erosion of American Democracy.* New York: Oxford University Press, 2011.

Hier, Sean P. and Josh Greenberg. *Surveillance: Power, Problems, and Politics.* Vancouver: UBC Press, 2009.

Keenan, Thomas P. *Technocreep: The Surrender of Privacy and the Capitalization of Intimacy.* New York: OR Books, 2014.

La Fave, Wayne R. *Search and Seizure: A Treatise on the Fourth Amendment.* 5ᵗʰ ed. Rochester, NY: Thomson West, 2012.

Monahan, Torin. *Surveillance and Security: Technological Politics and Power in Everyday Life.* New York: Routledge, 2006.

Nelson, Lisa S. *America Identified.* Cambridge, MA: The MIT Press, 2011.

Orwell, George. *Nineteen Eighty-four: A Novel.* New York: Harcourt, Brace, 1949.

Petersen, Julie K. *Understanding Surveillance Technologies: Spy Devices, Privacy, History & Applications.* Boca Raton: Auerbach Publications, 2007.

Posner, Richard A. *Not a Suicide Pact: The Constitution in a Time of National Emergency.* New York: Oxford University Press, 2006.

———. "Privacy, Surveillance, and Law." *The University of Chicago Law Review* 75, no. 1 (2008): 245–60. http://www.jstor.org/stable/20141907.

Slobogin, Christopher. *Privacy at Risk: The New Government Surveillance and the Fourth Amendment.* Chicago: University of Chicago Press, 2007.

Solove, Daniel J. *Nothing to Hide: The False Tradeoff between Privacy and Security.* New Haven: Yale University Press, 2011.

———. *The Digital Person: Technology and Privacy in the Information Age.* New York: New York University Press, 2004.

Turkington, Richard C., and Anita L. Allen. *Privacy Law: Cases and Materials.* St. Paul, MN: West Group, 2002.

United States. Congress. Senate. Committee on the Judiciary. Subcommittee on Privacy, Technology, and the Law. *What Facial Recognition Technology Means for Privacy and Civil Liberties: Hearing Before the Subcommittee On Privacy, Technology and the Law of the Committee On the Judiciary, United States Senate, One Hundred Twelfth Congress, Second Session, July 18, 2012.* Washington: U.S. Government Printing Office, 2012.

Warren, Samuel D. and Louis D. Brandeis. "The Right to Privacy." *Harvard Law Review* 4, no. 5 (1890): 193–220. doi: 10.2307/1321160.

Webb, Maureen. *Illusions of Security: Global Surveillance and Democracy in the Post-9/11 World.* San Francisco: City Lights Books, 2007.

Westin, Alan F. *Privacy and Freedom.* New York: Atheneum, 1970.

Whitaker, Reginald. *The End of Privacy: How Total Surveillance Is Becoming a Reality.* New York: New Press, 1999.

Woodward, John D. Jr. and Arroyo Center. *Super Bowl Surveillance: Facing Up to Biometrics.* Santa Monica, CA: RAND Arroyo Center, 2001.

Woodward, John D. Jr. Rand Corporation and United States Congress. House Committee on Government Reform, Subcommittee on the District of Columbia. *Privacy Vs. Security: Electronic Surveillance in the Nation's Capital.* Santa Monica, CA: RAND, 2002.

Woodward, John D. Jr. Virginia State Crime Commission and Rand Corporation. *Biometrics: A Look at Facial Recognition.* Santa Monica, CA: RAND, 2003.

Zoufal, Donald R. "Someone to Watch Over Me?: Privacy and Governance Strategies for CCTV and Emerging Surveillance Technologies." Master's thesis, Naval Postgraduate School, 2008. http://handle.dtic.mil/100.2/ADA480074.

Made in the USA
San Bernardino, CA
13 August 2019